DANCING COLORS

Secrets and Techniques for Fluid Acrylic
Painting Beginners

Audrey Walter

1

Table of Contents

CHAPTER ONE

INTRODUCTION

Might it be said that you are prepared to plunge into the universe of liquid acrylic painting? This charming work of art has gotten the hearts of specialists and craftsmanship lovers all around the planet, offering constant inventive potential outcomes with its remarkable pouring strategies and enamoring results. I will direct you through the essentials of liquid acrylic painting, from getting a handle on the creative verbalization and significant materials to overpowering crucial and critical level techniques. So get your paintbrush and might we at any point leave on this impressive excursion together!

SHORT DYNAMIC OF LIQUID SHOW-STOPPER

Liquid acrylic painting is a show-stopper that requires an impression of materials and strategies. This book gives direction on fundamental materials, like paints, pouring mediums and surfaces, imperative for best in class liquid acrylic strategies, and tips for bring about collection theory and thickness control. Plus, exploring regular issues. Trial and error with pouring mediums and added substances can assist with accomplishing required paint stream and surface for remarkable creative indications.

UNDERSTANDING LIQUID ACRYLIC PAINTING

Liquid acrylic painting, by and large called acrylic pouring or liquid workmanship, is a framework that integrates pouring and controlling acrylic paint on a material to make wonderful, The significance of liquid paint workmanship, likewise recommended as liquid craftsmanship painting, lies in its simplicity and the marbling impact made by the trading of collections, going with it an outstanding decision for informed authorities, all things being equal. Wisdom anticipates a critical part in accomplishing the best consequences of this imaginative work.

Getting the paint prior making pours guarantees that it has the right thickness for spilling and pouring, decreasing the probability of paint films breaking and tearing. It is also basic for permit abundance paint in cups to dry out totally going before discarding it in the real way.

While working with liquid acrylic paint, moving the material works with the development of paint, making novel models. Layering the paints and understanding the properties of the materials utilized are pivotal variables in making clearly spellbinding liquid craftsmanship masterpieces. With a strong handle of the basics, you'll be especially gone to prevailing at liquid acrylic painting.

KEY MATERIALS FOR LIQUID ACRYLIC PAINTING

Before you start your liquid acrylic painting experience, it is imperative for accumulate the focal materials. You will require acrylic paints, a pouring medium, and a fitting material or surface. The right blend of these materials will guarantee useful material information and staggering outcomes.

In the going with parts, we will jump further into the particulars of picking the right acrylic paints, picking a reasonable pouring medium, and picking the best material or surface for your liquid craftsmanship show-stopper.

CHAPTER TWO

PICKING THE RIGHT ACRYLIC PAINTS

The way in to a convincing liquid acrylic painting lies in picking the right sort of acrylic paint. For pouring, acrylic paints with the right consistency, as delicate body or liquid acrylics, are proposed. Delicate Body Acrylic Paints, Acrylic Inks, and understudy grade acrylic paints like Winsor and Newton Galeria, Daler Rowney Framework 3, and Sennelier Sensible are legitimate decisions. The proposed consistency of acrylic paint for pouring is honey-like. Be cautious not to add over the top water to your acrylic paint going before integrating your pouring medium, as this could chip away at the probability of the pour not succeeding. Touchy Body, High Stream, or Liquid Acrylic Paints routinely have a consistency running between that of milk (ink and high stream) and significant cream (delicate body and liquid).

PICKING A POURING MEDIUM

A pouring medium is a significant piece of liquid acrylic painting, as it offers various advantages when utilized for acrylic pouring, for example, giving consistency, assortment thickness, and paint stick to the material surface. Also, it assists with frustrating breaking of the paint surface by virtue of the speedy dispersing of water.

For ideal outcomes, picking an acrylic pouring medium that further creates paint stream and ruins breaking, for example, Liquitex Pouring Medium or Floetrol is proposed.

While joining acrylic paint and pouring medium, utilizing a 1:1 proportion is recommended. This degree guarantees that the paint has the huge consistency for pouring, permitting you to accomplish the best impacts and procedures in your liquid workmanship craftsmanship's. Examining different streets concerning different pouring mediums and degrees will assist you with tracking down the best blend for your incredible inventive style.

PICKING A MATERIAL OR SURFACE

Picking the right material or surface for your liquid acrylic painting is correspondingly by and large around as basic as picking the right paint and pouring medium. An organized and reasonable choice, as extended material or painting sheets, ought to be chosen to guarantee the best outcomes. Any level surface prepared with a fitting show for acrylic painting is reasonable for acrylic pour painting. Gesso is a central that can manage the stream and adherence of the paint. Applying gesso to your material or surface going before pouring guarantees that the paint sticks appropriately, accomplishing more excited areas of strength for and of craftsmanship. It is additionally conceivable to utilize liquid acrylic painting on surfaces, yet it is central to see that acrylics can make the surface areas of strength for become they solidify. Acrylic surface paints and a surface medium can be utilized to remain mindful of flexibility. To guarantee an even paint film on an excessively long material, you can maintain the rear of the material with a card or another fittingly surveyed level thing or utilize wooden material keys to expand the type of the material. Setting up your material or surface definitively will set the establishment for an effective liquid acrylic painting.

KEY LIQUID ACRYLIC STRATEGY

Now that you better handle the materials expected for liquid acrylic painting, this second is the best an open door to investigate several focal strategies. The standard pour, messy pour, and swipe frameworks are juvenile satisfying and versatile liquid workmanship techniques you can examine different streets regarding. Every strategy offers a working out way to agreement with controlling paint on the material, permitting you to make staggering models and plans. Might we at some point plunge into every strategy and find how they can restore your liquid acrylic syntheses!

CONVENTIONAL POUR

The customary pour is the most central procedure in acrylic pouring, including pouring different paint tones onto a material. This method gives you more command over the arrangement and mixing of varieties, making it ideal for those new to liquid acrylic painting and hoping to investigate acrylic pouring procedures.

To make a customary paint pouring, pour individual tones onto the material and control them to make wanted designs. You can utilize brushes, range blades, or even your fingers to move the paint and make different impacts.

The conventional pour is a phenomenal beginning stage for fledglings, offering a basic yet compelling method for investigating the universe of acrylic pour canvases and liquid acrylic painting.

GRIMY POUR

One more well known procedure in liquid acrylic painting is the filthy pour, which includes layering numerous varieties in a solitary cup and pouring them onto the material to make an exceptional and dynamic fine art. The outcome is a marbled impact, with colors intermixing and making eye-getting designs. While executing the grimy pour strategy, it is fundamental to painstakingly layer the varieties in the cup, taking into account the shade thickness and how each variety will associate with the others. When the varieties are poured onto the material, you can control the paint by shifting the material, utilizing devices, or in any event, consolidating added substances, for example, silicone oil to make cells in the paint. Exploring different avenues regarding various varieties, pouring strategies and added substances is vital to dominating the filthy pour strategy and accomplishing staggering outcomes.

SWIPE PROCEDURE

The swipe procedure is another fundamental liquid acrylic painting technique that includes pouring layers of paint and utilizing an instrument to swipe across the surface, delivering exceptional examples. This procedure can make striking impacts, like cells, lines, and variety angles, adding profundity and interest to your liquid acrylic compositions.

To execute the swipe method, start by pouring layers of paint onto your material or surface. Then, utilize a device, for example, a range blade, charge card, or even a piece of paper, to tenderly swipe across the paint's surface, making the ideal examples and impacts. The swipe method offers vast opportunities for trial and error, permitting you to foster your own one of a kind style and make dazzling liquid acrylic works of art.

CHAPTER THREE

HIGH LEVEL LIQUID ACRYLIC METHODS

As you progress in your liquid acrylic painting venture, you might be anxious to investigate further developed procedures to make many-sided and enthralling plans. Tree whirl, Dutch pour, and making cells with silicone oil are instances of cutting edge liquid acrylic strategies that can raise your work of art and challenge your abilities.

How about we dive further into these methods and find how they can add an additional dash of refinement to your liquid workmanship manifestations.

Tree Whirl

The tree whirl is a high level liquid acrylic painting procedure that includes pouring different paint tones onto a material and afterward utilizing an instrument, like a brush or stick, to control the paint and art a tree-like example. This strategy permits you to make mind boggling, natural plans that impersonate the normal magnificence of a tree. To execute the tree whirl procedure, start by pouring paint in a roundabout movement onto your material or surface. Then, utilize a device, like a brush or stick, to control the paint and make a tree-like example. This procedure requires some training and persistence, yet the outcome is a dazzling, stand-out liquid acrylic painting.

Dutch Pour

The Dutch pour strategy is one higher level liquid work of art technique that includes pouring numerous paint tones onto a material and afterward using a blow dryer or air control to get the paint across the material, making natural examples. This method is ideal for specialists hoping to make unique, liquid plans with a feeling of development and energy. Start by pouring your picked colors onto the material exclusively or utilizing a messy pour method. Then, utilize a blow dryer or other device to control the paint, moving it in different headings to make the ideal examples and impacts. Make certain to work with watchfulness and control, as the strong air from the blow dryer can undoubtedly make the paint splatter or move in accidental ways. The Dutch pour strategy offers an extraordinary method for making dynamic, liquid workmanship pieces that enamor and rouse.

MAKING CELLS WITH SILICONE OIL

Making cells with silicone oil is a high level liquid acrylic painting procedure that includes integrating a couple of drops of silicone oil into the paint prior to pouring it onto the material. This procedure works with the production of cells in the paint, which can be controlled to shape outwardly engaging examples and surfaces. To make cells with silicone oil, add a couple of drops of silicone oil to your paint combinations and mix tenderly. Be careful not to over mix, which can cause the silicone oil to separate and lose its cell-framing properties. When the silicone oil is consolidated, pour the paint onto your material and utilize your picked method to control the paint and make the ideal cell designs. This procedure might require practice and trial and error however the outcomes can be dazzling and one of a kind.

TIPS FOR PROGRESS IN LIQUID ACRYLIC PAINTING

Since you have a strong comprehension of the different liquid acrylic painting methods, remembering a few hints for progress is significant. Figuring out variety hypothesis and choice, controlling paint consistency, and permitting more than adequate drying and relieving time are fundamental in making liquid craftsmanship show-stoppers. In the accompanying segments, we will investigate these tips in additional detail, furnishing you with the apparatuses and information expected to succeed in your liquid acrylic painting venture.

VARIETY HYPOTHESIS AND CHOICE

Variety hypothesis and choice are urgent for making outwardly engaging liquid acrylic compositions. Understanding how tones communicate with one another and utilizing the variety wheel to make amicable variety blends will assist you with accomplishing striking and adjusted organizations. While choosing colors for your liquid acrylic painting, think about tint, worth, and immersion factors. Your own inclination, wanted temperament, and by and large structure of your piece ought to likewise be thought about while picking tones. Exploring different avenues regarding different variety blends and consolidating integral and differentiating tones will assist you with fostering your imaginative style and make outwardly staggering liquid craftsmanship pieces. Figuring out variety hypothesis and choosing suitable tones for your liquid acrylic works of art is fundamental for accomplishing eye-getting and amicable outcomes. By excelling at variety determination, you'll be well headed to making liquid acrylic compositions that really stick out.

Thickness Control

Thickness control is fundamental for accomplishing your liquid acrylic works of art's ideal paint stream and surface. Trying different things with various pouring mediums and added substances, for example, water or silicone oil can assist you with finding the ideal equilibrium of thickness for your novel artwork style. It's vital to figure out the parts of your work of art, like speed and space, and to use appropriate materials, similar to the right acrylic paints and pouring medium. By dominating thickness control, you can make liquid acrylic compositions with different impacts and procedures, permitting your creative vision to show some major signs of life on the material.

Drying and Relieving Time

Permitting adequate drying and restoring time for your liquid acrylic artistic creations is significant for the life span and nature of your work of art. By and large, drying times for liquid acrylic artworks are 24-72 hours, and relieving times are 7-14 days. It's vital for be patient and oppose the impulse to rush the drying system, as this can prompt breaking, twisting, or different issues in the last piece.

To guarantee the best outcomes, keep your liquid acrylic canvases in a very much ventilated region, away from direct daylight, and permit them to dry and fix totally prior to contacting or fixing them. Permitting more than adequate drying and restoring time will guarantee that your liquid acrylic works of art stay dynamic and lovely for a really long time.

INVESTIGATING NORMAL LIQUID ACRYLIC PAINTING ISSUES

Similarly as with any work of art, liquid acrylic painting presents difficulties and issues. Issues like air pockets, sloppy varieties, and lopsided surfaces can emerge during painting. Notwithstanding, with a few information and practice, you can investigate these issues and keep on making shocking, liquid workmanship. Air pockets can shape in your liquid acrylic artworks in the event that the pouring blend is fomented excessively or on the other hand on the off chance that the pouring medium doesn't remove bubbles proficiently. To forestall bubbles, make a pouring blend in with negligible fomentation and permit it to remain prior to utilizing it. Utilizing a pouring medium that removes bubbles effectively can likewise assist with diminishing this issue. Sloppy tones can happen when varieties blend a lot on the material, bringing about a dull and unappealing appearance. To stay away from sloppy varieties, cautiously layer your paint tones and utilize a variety wheel to choose corresponding or differentiating colors that won't mix. Figuring out variety hypothesis and choosing suitable tones for your liquid acrylic artworks will assist with limiting the gamble of sloppy varieties.

Lopsided surfaces can result from unlevel drying, prompting a debilitated paint film. To guarantee level drying, put your material on a totally level surface and utilize a soul level to affirm. By resolving these normal issues, you can keep on making liquid acrylic artworks that are outwardly engaging and liberated from blemishes.

Outline

Taking everything into account, liquid acrylic painting is an astonishing and adaptable artistic expression that offers unending innovative potential outcomes. You can make staggering, exceptional fluid craftsmanship show-stoppers by understanding the essentials of liquid acrylic painting, choosing appropriate materials, and dominating fundamental and high level methods. As you keep testing and filling in your liquid acrylic painting venture, make sure to embrace the cycle, gain from your slip-ups, and, above all, have some good times! The universe of fluid workmanship is hanging tight for you to do something significant.

CHAPTER FOUR

WHAT IS LIQUID ACRYLIC PAINTING

Liquid acrylic painting, otherwise called acrylic pouring, is a sort of theoretical craftsmanship including pouring meager, fluid acrylic paint onto a material for fascinating natural shapes. The paint utilized is profoundly pigmented and has the consistency of weighty cream, making it a lot more slender than weighty body paint. This sort of painting is turning out to be progressively famous because of its novel and unusual outcomes. It is an incredible method for investigating tone and surface, and can be utilized to make dazzling show-stoppers. It is likewise moderately simple to pick up, making it an incredible action.

What is the contrast between acrylic paint and liquid acrylic paint?

Liquid acrylics have a more slender consistency than conventional weighty body acrylics, making them appropriate for detail work, staining, watercolor methods and dry-brush work. Weighty body acrylics hold brushstrokes and work with variety blending and mixing.

Could you at any point do liquid workmanship with acrylic paint?

Indeed, liquid workmanship can be made with acrylic paint. The strategy includes pouring the paint onto a material and shifting the composition surface to accomplish wanted plans. It's an agreeable and remunerating action for all expertise levels.

How would you make liquid acrylic paint?

To make your own liquid acrylics, track down a reasonable compartment, add medium/water, blend 'typical' acrylic paint, utilize a pipe whenever wanted, and combine everything as one completely. At the point when you're finished, clean the spout and guarantee it has an impermeable seal.

What is liquid pouring?

Liquid pouring, otherwise called acrylic pouring, is a liquid painting procedure used to make unique workmanship by pouring flimsy layers of fluid acrylic paint onto a material. The paint moves and spreads unreservedly, making natural shapes for novel and fascinating show-stoppers.

What materials do you really want for acrylic pouring?

They are the fundamental materials that you really want to have for acrylic paint pouring. The variety you pick is altogether dependent upon you however remember the 'body' of the paint you use. The outcome of your pour still up in the air by the consistency of your acrylic paint. You can pick Liquitex proficient acrylic inks to begin. These very liquid tones contain super-fine colors suspended in a best in class emulsion. Speedy drying, super durable, water-safe, and non-obstructing, they're great for different procedures.

One more simple decision for amateurs is Demco master liquid acrylic paint which is made utilizing the best unrefined components accessible making these self-evening out paints and can be utilized as watercolor paints. Tri-Craftsmanship Individual Rheotech Acrylic Paint is likewise a decent choice since this understudy grade acrylic paint likewise has rich and serviceable consistency. Additionally, it has magnificent grip and won't chip, break or separate in the container.

Pouring Medium

Acrylic paint pouring medium is a material that guides in the consistency of acrylic paints by permitting them to stream all the more unreservedly. Blending acrylic paint pouring medium with acrylic paints changes them, permitting you to cause awesome acrylic to pour craftsmanship. Utilizing an expert acrylic pouring medium as opposed to a more affordable choice lessens the probability of imperfections creating when your pour dries. Liquitex Acrylic Pouring Medium is one of the most well known pouring mediums among craftsmen which has a unique equation that gives the most consistent outcomes when utilized with pour painting strategies.

Painting Grounds

Acrylic pour painting should be possible on practically any level surface that has been appropriately arranged for acrylic painting. A few specialists like to deal with customary extended materials, while others pick more straightforward to-store material sheets or painting boards. In any case, the most ideal choice to work with acrylic pouring paint ought to be Apollon Go trick fluid craftsmanship board with basswood cots and painting surface produced using Russian birch which is a striking choice to masterpiece on material. It is great for pouring medium and sap.

HOW TO DO ACRYLIC PAINT POURING

Pour painting is chaotic, and it requires a couple of days for the paint to fix, so the work area should be completely ready prior to beginning. You need to guarantee a clean and residue free work area to stay away from residue and pet hair getting into the wet paint. Moreover, you likewise must have a level, durable surface which is expected for the painting to flawlessly dry. In the event that you have pets or small kids, you really want a room with an entryway that can be shut so they don't coincidentally contact or tip your fine art.

Plan pouring surfaces

As referenced before, the material is presently famously utilized as a surface for pouring. You ought to pick the prescribed one to do your pouring workmanship to guarantee the ideal outcomes. A little tip is to apply a layer of gesso (an acrylic preliminary if utilizing an unprimed material) to your material to make it simpler for the paint to stick. Every use of gesso requires around 45 minutes to dry, so begin this venture early. When the gesso is dry, you can cover the rear of your material so it doesn't get covered with paint during the pouring system.

Blend your paints

Blending acrylic paint for pouring requirements a ton of persistence and detail. You will figure out how to blend acrylic paint for pouring assuming you follow these means. Put some acrylic, right off the bat, paint in a cup or holder of your decision, and afterward pour in a similar amount or two times as a significant part of the pouring medium, contingent upon the pouring medium utilized. Then, cautiously join each of the fixings until they structure a uniform acrylic combination. It ought to have the consistency of fluid honey. Assuming that the acrylic combination is excessively slim, gather extra water and mix everything into a single unit once more. In any case, utilizing a lot of water can break the acrylic polymer particle so it is prescribed not to utilize over 30% of water in the blend. Assuming you maintain that your canvases should have cells, add 1-2 drops of silicone oil and blend it in generally. At long last, consider some time for any air pockets to ascend to the outer layer of these blends. Assuming that you begin painting right away, you'll wind up with scars out of control.

Begin pouring

Craftsmen are continuously testing and growing new pouring strategies. In the event that you're simply getting everything rolling, it's urgent to at first gain proficiency with a few crucial strategies.

There are 2 fundamental acrylic pouring methods as follows:

Customary pouring

Delicately pour each tone onto your material or load up each in turn. This technique gives you more command over the position of your variety.

You can add sprinkles of variety any place you think the arrangement calls for them.

Get the material after you've applied your paint and delicately slant it to urge the paint to create interesting examples and puddles. Permitting the paint to dribble down the sides of your synthesis will give it a cleaned appearance.

Filthy Pouring

Take one clean paper cup and continuously layer tones from various cups into it. The manner in which you empty your paints into the cup will influence how they look when they're poured onto your material. To perceive what the area means for your pores, have a go at pouring varieties down the internal side of the cup or straight into the middle. The manner in which it pours will contrast contingent upon how rapidly the variety is presented. On the off chance that you add tone to the cup too quickly, it will sink to the base. The variety will settle at the highest point of the cup in the event that you add it gradually. To make various kinds of pours, try different things with fluctuated velocities and areas. Then, at that point, pour the varieties straightforwardly onto the material from the cup. You can do this in any example you need, as long as the material is reasonably similarly covered. Get the material and cautiously slant it once the tones have been all additional. Shifting permits the paint to fill in the holes and can be all used to make one of a kind examples.

Finish the edges

Check out every one of the four lines for any areas that aren't painted. Smooth some paint onto those parts with a range blade or a woodcraft stick. You can utilize any extra paint from your cups.

Try not to worry about getting the edges amazing on the grounds that, as found in the makes underneath, you can apply final details once the work of art is totally dry.

FAQs

How to thin acrylic paint for pouring?

Not at all like different kinds of painting, you could not blend acrylic at any point paint with water to weaken it since acrylic paint is water-solvent, implying that it is broken up by water. All things considered, you need to add a pouring medium that will assist your paint with streaming while at the same time keeping the cement properties of your paints.

Is it conceivable to sell acrylic pour artworks?

There are a few settings where you might sell your acrylic pour craftsmanship, yet it's not generally as basic as it shows up. Most of individuals know nothing about the time and assets expected to make your acrylic pour compositions. So do it for the fun of making, not for bringing in cash. Besides, to offer acrylic pour canvases to potential craftsmanship financial backers or gatherers, you ought to select cautiously proficient materials. The bad quality items can bring about breaking and stripping which lessen the artistic creation's worth after some time.

THE END